FRANCIS FRITH'S

VICTORIAN AND EDWARDIAN DORSET

Happy Birthday Robbie

25th November 2013

THE FRANCIS FRITH COLLECTION

www.francisfrith.com

Photographic Memories

Francis Frith's
Victorian and
Edwardian Dorset

Keith Howell

First published in the United Kingdom in 2001 by
The Francis Frith Collection

Paperback Edition
ISBN 978-1-84589-480-1

British Library Cataloguing in Publication Data

Francis Frith's Victorian and Edwardian Dorset
Keith Howell

The Francis Frith Collection
Unit 6, Oakley Business Park, Wylye Road,
Dinton, Wiltshire SP3 5EU
Tel: +44 (0) 1722 716 376
Email: info@francisfrith.co.uk
www.francisfrith.com

Printed and bound in Great Britain

Front Cover: Netherbury, Haymaking by St Mary's Church 1912 65068t

The colour-tinting is for illustrative purposes only, and is not intended to be historically accurate

Contents

Francis Frith: *Victorian Pioneer*

FRANCIS FRITH, Victorian founder of the world-famous photographic archive, was a complex and multi-talented man. A devout Quaker and a highly successful Victorian businessman, he was both philosophic by nature and pioneering in outlook.

By 1855 Francis Frith had already established a wholesale grocery business in Liverpool, and sold it for the astonishing sum of £200,000, which is the equivalent today of over £15,000,000. Now a multi-millionaire, he was able to indulge his passion for travel. As a child he had pored over travel books written by early explorers, and his fancy and imagination had been stirred by family holidays to the sublime mountain regions of Wales and Scotland. 'What a land of spirit-stirring and enriching scenes and places!' he had written. He was to return to these scenes of grandeur in later years to 'recapture the thousands of vivid and tender memories', but with a different purpose. Now in his thirties, and captivated by the new science of photography, Frith set out on a series of pioneering journeys to the Nile regions that occupied him from 1856 until 1860.

Intrigue and Adventure

He took with him on his travels a specially-designed wicker carriage that acted as both dark-room and sleeping chamber. These far-flung journeys were packed with intrigue and adventure. In his life story, written when he was sixty-three, Frith tells of being held captive by bandits, and of fighting 'an awful midnight battle to the very point of surrender with a deadly pack of hungry, wild dogs'. Sporting flowing Arab costume, Frith arrived at Akaba by camel seventy years before Lawrence, where he encountered 'desert princes and rival sheikhs, blazing with jewel-hilted swords'.

During these extraordinary adventures he was assiduously exploring the desert regions bordering the Nile and patiently recording the antiquities and peoples with his camera. He was the first photographer to venture beyond the sixth cataract. Africa was still the mysterious 'Dark Continent', and Stanley and Livingstone's historic meeting was a decade into the future. The conditions for picture taking confound belief. He laboured for hours in his wicker dark-room in the sweltering heat of the desert, while the volatile chemicals fizzed dangerously in their trays. Often he was forced to work in remote tombs and caves where conditions were cooler. Back in London he exhibited his photographs and was 'rapturously cheered' by members of the Royal Society. His reputation as

a photographer was made overnight. An eminent modern historian has likened their impact on the population of the time to that on our own generation of the first photographs taken on the surface of the moon.

Venture of a Life-Time

Characteristically, Frith quickly spotted the opportunity to create a new business as a specialist publisher of photographs. He lived in an era of immense and sometimes violent change. For the poor in the early part of Victoria's reign work was a drudge and the hours long, and people had precious little free time to enjoy themselves. Most had no transport other than a cart or gig at their disposal, and had not travelled far beyond the boundaries of their own town or village. However,

by the 1870s, the railways had threaded their way across the country, and Bank Holidays and half-day Saturdays had been made obligatory by Act of Parliament. All of a sudden the ordinary working man and his family were able to enjoy days out and see a little more of the world.

With characteristic business acumen, Francis Frith foresaw that these new tourists would enjoy having souvenirs to commemorate their days out. In 1860 he married Mary Ann Rosling and set out with the intention of photographing every city, town and village in Britain. For the next thirty years he travelled the country by train and by pony and trap, producing fine photographs of seaside resorts and beauty spots that were keenly bought by millions of Victorians. These prints were painstakingly pasted into family albums and pored over during the dark nights of winter, rekindling precious memories of summer excursions.

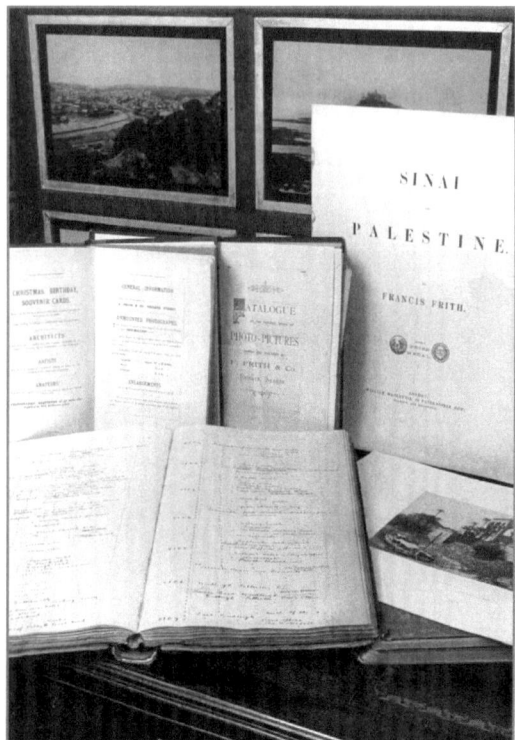

The Rise of Frith & Co

Frith's studio was soon supplying retail shops all over the country. To meet the demand he gathered about him a small team of photographers, and published the work of independent artist-photographers of the calibre of Roger Fenton and Francis Bedford. In order to gain some understanding of the scale of Frith's business one only has to look at the catalogue issued by Frith & Co in 1886: it runs to some 670 pages, listing not only many thousands of views of the British Isles but also many photographs of most European countries, and China, Japan, the USA and Canada – note the sample page shown above from the hand-written *Frith & Co* ledgers detailing pictures taken. By 1890 Frith had created the greatest specialist photographic publishing company in the world, with over 2,000 outlets – more than the combined number that Boots and W H Smith have today! The picture on the right shows the *Frith & Co* display board at Ingleton in the Yorkshire Dales. Beautifully constructed with mahogany frame and gilt inserts, it could display up to a dozen local scenes.

Postcard Bonanza

The ever-popular holiday postcard we know today took many years to develop. In 1870 the Post Office issued the first plain cards, with a pre-printed stamp on one face. In 1894 they allowed other publishers' cards to be sent through the mail with an attached adhesive halfpenny stamp. Demand grew rapidly, and in 1895 a new size of postcard was permitted called the court card, but there was little room for illustration. In 1899, a year after Frith's death, a new card measuring 5.5 x 3.5 inches became the standard format, but it was not until 1902 that the divided back came into being, with address and message on one face and a full-size illustration on the other. *Frith & Co* were in the vanguard of postcard development, and Frith's sons Eustace and Cyril continued their father's monumental task, expanding the number of views offered to the public and recording more and more places in Britain, as the coasts and countryside were opened up to mass travel.

Francis Frith died in 1898 at his villa in Cannes, his great project still growing. The archive he created continued in business for another seventy years. By 1970 it contained over a third of a million pictures of 7,000 cities, towns and villages. The massive photographic record Frith has left to us stands as a living monument to a special and very remarkable man.

Frith's Archive: *A Unique Legacy*

FRANCIS FRITH'S legacy to us today is of immense significance and value, for the magnificent archive of evocative photographs he created provides a unique record of change in 7,000 cities, towns and villages throughout Britain over a century and more. Frith and his fellow studio photographers revisited locations many times down the years to update their views, compiling for us an enthralling and colourful pageant of British life and character.

We tend to think of Frith's sepia views of Britain as nostalgic, for most of us use them to conjure up memories of places in our own lives with which we have family associations. It often makes us forget that to Francis Frith they were records of daily life as it was actually being lived in the cities, towns and villages of his day. The Victorian age was one of great and often bewildering change for ordinary people, and though the pictures evoke an impression of slower times, life was as busy and hectic as it is today.

We are fortunate that Frith was a photographer of the people, dedicated to recording the minutiae of everyday life. For it is this sheer wealth of visual data, the painstaking chronicle of changes in dress, transport, street layouts, buildings, housing, engineering and landscape that captivates us so much today. His remarkable images offer us a powerful link with the past and with the lives of our ancestors.

Today's Technology

Computers have now made it possible for Frith's many thousands of images to be accessed almost instantly. In the Frith archive today, each photograph is carefully 'digitised' then stored on a CD Rom. Frith archivists can locate a single photograph amongst thousands within seconds. Views can be catalogued and sorted under a variety of categories of place and content to the immediate benefit of researchers.

Inexpensive reference prints can be created for them at the touch of a mouse button, and a wide range of books and other printed materials assembled and published for a wider, more general readership - in the next twelve months over a hundred Frith local history titles will be published! The day-to-day workings of the archive are very different from how they were in Francis Frith's time: imagine the herculean task of sorting through eleven tons of glass negatives as Frith had to do to locate a particular sequence of pictures! Yet the

See Frith at www.francisfrith.com

archive still prides itself on maintaining the same high standards of excellence laid down by Francis Frith, including the painstaking cataloguing and indexing of every view.

It is curious to reflect on how the internet now allows researchers in America and elsewhere greater instant access to the archive than Frith himself ever enjoyed. Many thousands of individual views can be called up on screen within seconds on one of the Frith internet sites, enabling people living continents away to revisit the streets of their ancestral home town, or view places in Britain where they have enjoyed holidays. Many overseas researchers welcome the chance to view special theme selections, such as transport, sports, costume and ancient monuments.

We are certain that Francis Frith would have heartily approved of these modern developments in imaging techniques, for he himself was always working at the very limits of Victorian photographic technology.

The Value of the Archive Today

Because of the benefits brought by the computer, Frith's images are increasingly studied by social historians, by researchers into genealogy and ancestory, by architects, town planners, and by teachers and schoolchildren involved in local history projects.

In addition, the archive offers every one of us an opportunity to examine the places where we and our families have lived and worked down the years. Highly successful in Frith's own era, the archive is now, a century and more on, entering a new phase of popularity.

The Past in Tune with the Future

Historians consider the Francis Frith Collection to be of prime national importance. It is the only archive of its kind remaining in private ownership and has been valued at a million pounds. However, this figure is now rapidly increasing as digital technology enables more and more people around the world to enjoy its benefits.

Francis Frith's archive is now housed in an historic timber barn in the beautiful village of Teffont in Wiltshire. Its founder would not recognize the archive office as it is today. In place of the many thousands of dusty boxes containing glass plate negatives and an all-pervading odour of photographic chemicals, there are now ranks of computer screens. He would be amazed to watch his images travelling round the world at unimaginable speeds through network and internet lines.

The archive's future is both bright and exciting. Francis Frith, with his unshakeable belief in making photographs available to the greatest number of people, would undoubtedly approve of what is being done today with his lifetime's work. His photographs, depicting our shared past, are now bringing pleasure and enlightenment to millions around the world a century and more after his death.

Victorian & Edwardian Dorset
- *An Introduction*

"Vor Do'set dear
Then gi'e woone cheer;
D'ye hear? Woone cheer."

That amiable parson/poet from Winterbourne Came, William Barnes, spent a substantial part of his life celebrating the pleasures and patterns of Dorset rural life in a string of dialect poems, like the one cited above. But, by the time of his death in 1886, these familiar rhythms were already undergoing significant change and, by the time his illustrious counterpart Thomas Hardy passed away at Dorchester in 1928, the innovations of 20th-century life had already begun to wreak their inexorable alterations on the face of the county.

It is possible that man had first trod the Dorset landscape around 150,000 years ago, for the earliest traces of human occupation date back to the Patheolithic period between the Ice Ages. With the retreat of the glaciers around 10,000 BC, the first residents, in the shape of Mesolithic hunters, arrived to be followed by Neolithic farmers whose long barrows and causewayed enclosures are still a recognisable feature of parts of the countryside. The Bronze Age 'Beaker People', who built the round barrows, were followed by the iron-using Celts; the

Dwr y Triges, or Durotriges as the invading Romans called them. It was these 'people near the tidal water' who gave Dorset its name.

The Romans, the Saxons, the Vikings and the Normans have all left their mark in the names of Dorset's towns and rivers, with the latter contributing equally enduring physical mementoes in the architecture of its beautiful churches and ecclesiastical heritage. By the time that invaluable document, the Domesday Book, was compiled in 1086, the county's population was in excess of 35,000, with the Church owning almost two-fifths of the land and the majority of the remainder under the control of the king and his Norman barons.

Throughout the Middle Ages, and even after the Reformation, the county continued to remain the domain of large landowners, many of them non-residents, which stamped a particular character on both its landscape and its society. While agriculture retained its primary importance, in particular sheep-farming and the wool and textile industry, the manufacture of ropes and sailcloth around Bridport and the quarrying of Portland and Purbeck stone also employed substantial segments of the Dorset labour force.

Along with these aspects of economic growth and development, other less welcome upheavals within society played their part. The Civil War especially brought much suffering and bloodshed to the county through divisions between towns and districts, as well as within families. Moreover,

Dorset lay as a kind of buffer region between the Royalist strongholds in the West Country and the Parliamentarians around London. Similarly, the Monmouth Rebellion and the subsequent Bloody Assize of Judge Jeffreys, along with the prosecution of the Tolpuddle Martyrs in the 19th century, are further evidence of the turbulence which affected the lives of Dorset's residents.

By the time Frith and his colleagues embarked on their pictorial quests within the county's boundaries in the early 19th century, the gross disparities between rich and poor had already been revealed in what was still a remarkably feudal society. The decline in the cloth trade and in agriculture had provoked widespread rioting in the 1830s, in protest against low wages, bad conditions and incredibly long hours of work. The formerly rich Newfoundland fishing trade had also diminished from its peak, although the stone-quarrying areas continued to prosper. At the same time, the miserable living conditions of many agricultural workers contrasted with the comparative wealth and affluence to be found in the Dorset towns, and more especially in the great houses on the estates of the principal landowners.

The coming of the railways in the 1850s, coupled with a further long period of agricultural depression from 1870 onwards, led to a population drift away from the small villages towards the expanding towns and resorts and even, in some cases, to overseas emigration. But overall, Dorset's

population continued to grow, from just fewer than 115,000 in 1801 to more than 184,000 in 1851, and within the next 50 years to more than 200,000. The holiday resorts such as Weymouth, Lyme Regis and, most prominently, Poole and Bournemouth with their adjacent suburbs, became the focal points for much new development. Many of the following pictures show this, and these places accounted for a major proportion of this population influx.

While William Barnes did not live to see the arrival of the motor vehicle, and its impact on the county, Thomas Hardy did, although even he could not have foreseen to what extent it would help to transform both Dorset's landscape and society in the latter part of the 20th century. Hardy's novels effectively convey the isolation of many of the county's villages and hamlets, and their inhabitants, and of the problems which travellers faced in making their journeys. The railways, which featured in his works and in a number of the photographs included here, had a tremendous effect on the towns and villages through which they passed and helped to promote both population expansion and local enterprises. But within a century, the iron roads underwent a savage process of excision, and surrendered to the hegemony of the automobile. Today, many of the villages and hamlets depicted

in these pages can, once again, only be reached by road, albeit of a more solid construction than existed in previous times.

The overwhelming influence which motor-transport has had on our way of life during the latter decades of the 20th century is all too clearly revealed by the photographs assembled here. The construction of motorways and bypasses has, in its wake, produced a commensurate expansion of new housing and other development, and contributed to the growth of the major Dorset towns. Along with this increased mobility and access, vast swathes of the county, particularly around the coastline, have been given over to unsightly caravan and mobile home sites. What is perhaps more remarkable is that so many of the scenes collected in these pages are, in contrast to similar works devoted to other counties, still recognisable to those familiar with their present-day appearance. Except in the case of some of the more urban subjects, the glorious beauties of the remoter areas of Dorset have been apparently relatively untouched by the passage and events of the last hundred years. No doubt William Barnes, confronted with the more humane and prosperous condition of Dorset's vastly increased population and with so much of its lovely landscape and buildings still intact, would find much to cheer about.

Bournemouth & Environs

It was the reorganisation of local government in 1973-4 which enlarged the Dorset county boundaries, adding Bournemouth, Christchurch, the parishes of St Leonards and St Ives, Hurn, and part of the parishes of Sopley and Christchurch East to its existing area. Although, therefore, not historically strictly within the definition of this book's title, these delightful photographs of turn-of-the-century Bournemouth and its suburbs fully merit their inclusion.

Bournemouth
From West Cliff 1887 19529
In 1861 the district of Bournemouth had a resident population of 1,707 people. By 1881 it had increased to almost 17,000; such was the rapid pace of development of the little village of Bourne as a resort. On the right is the (then new) 950-foot iron pier which was opened on 11 August 1880, replacing an earlier wooden structure destroyed by gales and the ravages of the teredo, or ship worm. The town's MP, Horace Davey, donated the clock for the tower at the pier entrance in 1882. To its right are some of the bathing huts at the end of the East Cliff Promenade. Between this road ascending the cliffs and the Bath Road are the Sydenham subscription Reading Rooms; one of the few amusements available to visitors at this time. Behind were the Corporation Baths. Across the Bath Road is the frontage of the Pier Hotel.

◄ **Bournemouth
The Square 1900** 45212
Not a regular square,
but a central meeting of
the ways between the
Pleasure Gardens. To
the left rises the spire
of the Richmond Hill
Congregational Church.
The offices of the Royal
Assurance Company are
housed in the white two-
storey building while
behind, on the right is
the Central Hotel. Next
door is the Mansion
Family Hotel, more
accurately described as
a boarding house.

◀ **Bournemouth**
The Club House c1871 5660
At the foot of West Club, and on the sands close to the pier, stood this single storey building which was the headquarters of the Westover Rowing Club. In what were described as its "commodious premises" were committee rooms, changing rooms, a buffet room and a billiard room. The adjacent huts were used for the storage of racing galleys, skiffs, and two- and four-oared boats. The building existed until the end of the Edwardian era.

▼ **Bournemouth**
The Gardens 1890 25502
The Mansion Family Hotel appears on the extreme left of this picture, taken from the top of Exeter Lane across the Pleasure Gardens. Next door is the National Provincial Bank branch, with the tailoring and foot-wear stores of Barnes further along the parade of shops. The spire of St Peter's Church, rising to 202 feet, was added to the building in 1879.

◀ **Bournemouth**
The Cab Rank 1900 45218x
Outside the Royal Assurance Office in The Square, a cabby waits for a fare. A contemporary guidebook to Bournemouth acidly commented "The fares here are, on paper, much the same as at other places, a shilling a mile, three shillings an hour and so forth; but in practice there are complaints of the charges made, and the number of cabs usually standing about idle would seem to show that the proprietors stand in their own light".

Bournemouth, In the Gardens 1900 45225x

Bournemouth, On The Bourne 1900 45223
The Pleasure Gardens with their scented pines and attractively laid out grounds were popular with people of all ages, at a time when fashion and social mores decreed that the human form should remain covered in public. This sylvan setting was as equally appealing as the beach for young and old alike, and the waters of the Bourne, tamed and enclosed, were an ideal place for children to sail their boats.

Bournemouth, The Arcade c1871 5511a
Henry Joy, a carpenter, builder and entrepreneur, who visualised it becoming a popular shopping precinct, built the Gervis Arcade in 1866. The venture became known as 'Joy's Folly', since it took seven years to complete and its roof was not finally glazed until 1873. In 1868, it was possible to rent a shop with accommodation here for the meagre sum of £40 p.a.

Boscombe, The Chine Hotel 1892 31377
Originally built by Sir Drummond Wolfe in the early 18th century and later extended, this luxury hotel with 80 rooms, three acres of gardens and its own well, was immensely popular with the leading stars of the variety theatre and music halls of the period, who stayed here while appearing in Bournemouth.

Boscombe, The Pier 1892 31379
Situated at the foot of Boscombe Chine, the 700-foot pier commanded good views along the cliffs on either hand. The pierhead was also a regular fishing station. The 15 covered shelters provided ample protection from the elements in inclement weather.

Boscombe, from the Pier 1906 55907
With the turret of the Chine Hotel, which served as a landmark for Channel shipping, prominent in the background, the elegant row of Victorian houses along Undercliffe Road bears tribute to the enduring popularity of this eastern suburb of Bournemouth for Edwardian holidaymakers. The delicate ironwork tracery of the pier seating, and a solitary bathing machine parked by the pier pavilion are further examples of Boscombe's Victorian origins.

Boscombe, The Park 1906 55912
The ornamental Yacht Pond at the seaward end of Boscombe Chine has proved to be an enduring attraction for juvenile navigators. The chine, which derives its name from the old English word 'cinn', a chink or fissure, extends half a mile inland from Boscombe pier, and contains a substantial number of the estimated 3 million pine trees in the region, whose resinous scent perfumes the air.

Southbourne, Fisherman's Walk 1908 61204
Fishermen from neighbouring hamlets who used it to make their way to the sea named this narrow path through the pines, leading from Southbourne Overcliff to The Grove. Below the cliffs, shoals of mackerel could be caught.

Southbourne ▶
The Beach and Cliffs
1908 61202
The long, sandy beach
leading eastwards to
Hengistbury Head
began to be developed
around 1870. The pier
was built of iron in
1881, and measured
300 feet in length by
30 feet wide. Although
expected to be able to
withstand the elements
on this exposed stretch
of coast, it was badly
damaged by gales in
the winter of 1900, and
was finally dismantled
by Bournemouth
Corporation shortly after
this picture was taken.

◄ **Southbourne
The Beach and Cliffs
1908** 61201

Southbourne, General View 1900 45066
In 1870, a Bournemouth physician, Dr. Thomas Compton, purchased 230 acres of land, including a mile of sea frontage for £3,000, and named the district Southbourne-on-Sea. The first house was built two years later, by Henry Reeves, a leader writer for 'The Times' and the editor of the 'Edinburgh Review'. By the turn of the century, many more substantial villas had taken root amongst this expanse of gorse.

Christchurch, The Priory Church 1900 45040
The Church, seen across the combined waters of the Avon and Stour on their way to the sea, is a commanding feature of the scenery. Roger Flambard, the Bishop of Durham and the king's trusted adviser, began this largely Norman building towards the end of the 11th century. After his death in 1128, further construction was undertaken in the 13th and 14th centuries, culminating in the building of the west tower in the 15th century. In the Dissolution of the monasteries by Henry VIII, the Priory was destroyed, but the church was handed over to the parish.

Christchurch, The Wick Ferry 1900 45044
The first ferry service linking Christchurch to the tiny hamlet of Wick across the River Stour commenced around 1800, and was established by Eli Miller, in whose family it remained until 1903. A farm worker, who had been incapacitated by injury, introduced the ferry from Wick in 1814. His employer, John Sloman of Wick House, provided him with a boat and land at the riverside. The original charge was a halfpenny each way, with villagers travelling free on the return journey.

Highcliffe
The Castle 1900 45060
This romantic 19th-century Gothic castle stands on the site of a
house belonging to the 3rd Earl of Bute, the unpopular minister
of George III. The fabric of this building incorporated some late
medieval stonework brought from the Grande Maison des Andelys
in Normandy. It was built by W J Donthorne for the eccentric
British ambassador Lord Stuart de Rothesay between 1830-1834,
at a time when Lady Stuart was occupied elsewhere looking after
her invalid father. On returning to Highcliffe, and finding that the
neat villa she had left had been transformed into a sprawling castle,
she sharply criticised her husband and the architect and wrote
"I wish the whole thing had fallen over the cliff".

Victorian & Edwardian Dorset: The West

Lyme Regis
The Harbour 1890 27359
The harbour of this little town at the south-western extremity of
the county is renowned for its curious curved stone breakwater
and quay, The Cobb, which was first erected in the reign of
Edward I. Refurbished and maintained over successive reigns, by
the time of Elizabeth its level of shipping was recorded as being
one-sixth of London's.

▼ **Lyme Regis, from the Cobb 1900** 45234
Nestling in a combe between two rocky hills, the tower of the parish church of
St Michael is clearly visible in this view of the town, taken from the Cobb, on which
the Duke of Monmouth landed on 11 June 1685. It was also the fictitious site
where Jane Austen's character Louisa Musgrove leapt to disaster in 'Persuasion'.
Lyme was a favourite resort of the novelist and her family who stayed here during
its hey-day as a popular Regency watering place for fashionable Bath society.

▼ **Lyme Regis, Broad Street 1900** 45243
With the waters of Lyme Bay visible beyond the Hillcliff grocery store further down
this steeply-sloping street, the pleasing 18th-century façades of the shops and
buildings frame this scene of late Victorian activity. On the right, a lady emerges
from the entrance of one of the town's drapers, with its window displaying a
selection of parasols and blouses.

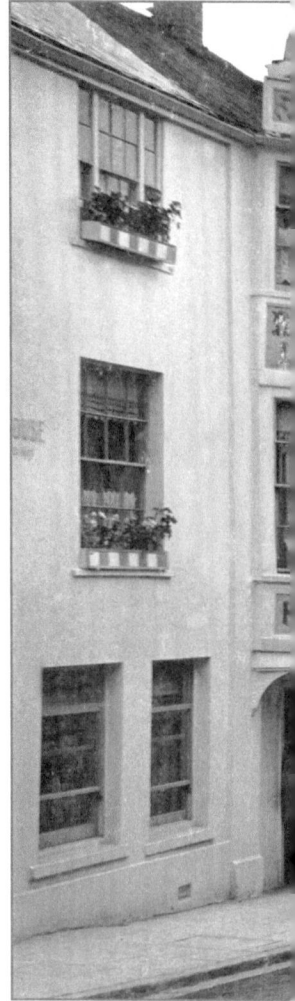

▲ **Lyme Regis
Broad Street 1909** 61627
Further along the street,
and almost a decade
later, an early motor car
is parked outside the
entrance of the Royal
Lion Hotel, which was
rebuilt in blue lias ashlar
after a devastating fire in
1844. In the distance the
grey shape of the Isle of
Portland, at the opposite
end of Lyme Bay, rises
from the sea.

◀ **Lyme Regis
The Parade from the
East 1907** 58091
The narrow esplanade,
constructed on land
reclaimed from the sea is
shown here, with the Cobb
out of view to the extreme
left. The steep and wooded
area behind the row of
bathing machines was the
site of a great landslip in
1839, when more than 40
acres of land moved to a
lower level.

Lyme Regis, Silver Street 1906 54530
A group of children are carefully posed for the photographer on this steeply-sloping street, watched by two ladies (their mothers?) from the nearby doorways, below the livery stables further up the hill. The children's cumbersome attire must have restricted their ability to play freely, and provides a marked contrast to today's fashions.

Lyme Regis
The Alexandra Hotel 1906 54533
This creeper-festooned building was originally constructed as
the Dower House for the first Countess of Poulett following her
husband's death in the 17th century. After passing through the
private ownership of several other families, it was transformed
into an hotel in 1901 by a consortium of four wealthy individuals
and named after the consort of Edward VII. A previous owner, the
Reverend Peake, earlier used the wooden pavilion to the left as a
science lecture room.

Charmouth, The Village 1890 27381

Charmouth, The Village 1900 46060

Two views of this charming seaside village street, taken a decade apart, but in which little appears to have changed. On the high road between Dorchester and Exeter, less than three miles east of Lyme Regis, Charmouth is reputed to have been one of the Roman stations and the later scene of fierce struggles between the Saxons and Danish invaders. The stuccoed Regency and Victorian villas lining this straight, climbing street however, bear witness to its popularity as a resort; and one whose scenic beauty was much admired by Jane Austen.

Morcombelake, General View 1904 52772

Morcombelake, Old Cottages 1904 52773

This discreet little settlement in the parish of Stanton St Gabriel occupies a web of small lanes on the south-facing slopes of Hardown Hill and derives its name from three Old English words: 'mor' (barren, swampy ground), 'cumb' (valley), and 'lacu' (stream). But travelling towards Charmouth in 1716, the poet John Gay penned the lines "through Bridport's stony lanes our route we take, And the proud steep descend to Morcomb's Lake", thus exposing subsequent generations of inhabitants to questions from puzzled visitors as to the location of this fabled mere.

Whitchurch Canonicorum The Village 1903

50491

Five miles from Bridport, and at the southern end of the Marshwood Vale, this small village appeared as Witancoercian in Alfred the Great's will, bequeathing it to his son Aethelward. But in 1240, the rectory was divided between the canons of Salisbury and those of Wells, resulting in the appended 'Canonicorum'. The Perpendicular tower of the early English church of St Candida and the Holy Cross rises above one of the impressive parish churches in the county, which houses a rare 16th-century stone shrine to St Wite.

Whitchurch Canonicorum The Village 1910
62270
One suspects that the four besmocked children eyeing the photographer and his equipment from their vantage point beneath the surprisingly truncated lamppost, had earlier been riding the small trolley cart, which is on the opposite side of the road, down the sloping village street.

Bettiscombe, General View 1904 52776
Looking south towards Lyme Bay, whose waters can be glimpsed on the right of the picture, the little hamlet of Bettiscombe sits amid the rolling fields and wooded countryside of the Marshwood Vale. The Perpendicular west tower of the Victorian church of St Stephen, in the right centre, stands near the 17th-century Manor House, built for John Pinney, who was vicar of Broadwindsor during the Cromwellian years. His son, Azariah, took part in the Monmouth Rebellion and was sentenced to be transported to the West Indies as a slave. He became a plantation owner andmade his fortune. In turn, his son became Chief Justice of Nevis and returned to Bettiscombe House around 1800.

Broadwindsor, The Village 1902 48445
This sizeable village nestles in a valley close to two notable landmarks: Lewesdon Hill (894 feet) and Pilsdon Pen, at 909 feet, the highest hill in Dorset. Sailors viewing them from off the coast at West Bay dubbed them 'the Cow and Calf'. The church of St John the Baptist, with its Perpendicular tower, stands on a terrace overlooking the village and boasted a peal of six bells, three of which were cast at least a century before the Reformation.

Stoke Abbot, The Village 1902 48443
In a valley on a road to nowhere, and six miles north of Bridport, this small collection of stone houses, the Norman church of St Mary (remodelled in the 13th century), and a pub, was originally part of the wealth enjoyed by the Abbey of Sherborne. While some of these buildings date from the 17th century, others bear inscriptions placing their construction, or modification, in the mid-18th century.

Netherbury, The Village 1902 48440
Standing outside the village Post Office on the left, the bewiskered elderly man leaning on two sticks and wearing a bowler hat was probably a figure of some status in the village, where there were a number of mills in the vicinity, processing flax for the fishing nets and ropes manufactured at nearby Bridport. Draped on the garden hedge of the adjoining two-storey brick house is an item of laundry laid out to dry amid the surrounding hollyhocks.

Netherbury, The Village 1902 48441
Set against the hillside and above the village buildings bordering the Brid, is the fine Perpendicular church of
St Mary which houses an alabaster monument of a 15th-century knight. There is also a brass mural in memory
of Admiral Sir Samuel Hood (of Nelson fame) and his two sailor brothers, all of whom were born in the parish.

Melplash, The Village 1907 58146
Only the feet of the carter are visible, as his horse stands patiently waiting while he unloads part of his wares
from the back of his wagon for delivery to the creeper-festooned cottages in this village on the main road linking
Bridport and Beaminster. In these Edwardian days, before motor transport supplanted the horse, these travelling
trades-men provided an essential service to outlying villages and homes.

Beaminster, General View 1907 58133
This tranquil view of this old market town, set amid rich grazing pastures, belies a turbulent history. The town was ravaged by fire during the Civil War, and was rebuilt by the Long Parliament. But two other conflagrations, in 1684 and 1781, destroyed the Market House and properties around the church. In 1685, following the failed Monmouth Rebellion and Judge Jeffrey's bloody Assize hearings at Dorchester, the butchered bodies of some of the 74 local men sentenced to death were suspended from the church tower.

Beaminster, St Mary's Church 1902 48423
The spectacular 16th century west tower of St Mary's Church, with its stockade of pinnacles, soars above the surrounding cottages and gardens. The church was repaired and restored in the late 19th century by William White, and a separate building called the Mort House was incorporated into the south side.

Beaminster, A Footpath 1907   58145x
An agricultural labourer pauses to smoke his pipe amid the wild flowers lining this narrow byway. Such Dorset men were always among the worst paid in Britain. His wage of 11 shillings a week in 1880 (when the national average wage was 14) had risen to only 16 shillings by the beginning of the First World War.

Toller Porcorum, The Village 1906 54554

Toller Porcorum, The Village 1906 54556
Here we are near the bed of a dried-up stream called the Toller, whose previous course is commemorated in the names of several neighbouring settlements. This is the only Dorset village whose name is in pig Latin. In 1259 it was known as Swynesthoire, in 1340 as Tolre Porcorum, and as Swyntoller in 1457 during a period when great herds of swine were bred here. But local residents have always referred to it as Great Toller, although its association with matters porcine continued through into the 19th century. The arrival of the railway as part of the Bridport branch line in 1857, prompted the building of a number of solid Victorian houses among the thatched cottages, over which the square embattled tower of the parish church of St Peter and St Andrew presides benignly.

Powerstock, The Village 1902 48417

That mobile monarch, King John, built a hunting lodge here in 1205, in what was the middle of the extensive Poorstock Forest. He was following in the footsteps of the Saxon king Athelstan whose own castle was sited on one of the green knolls in this valley, and of the Durotriges, a tribe who inhabited the area before the Roman invasion. The church of St Mary stands on another knoll, crowning the village, whose buildings occupy lesser prominences.

Loders, The Village & Church 1903 50495

This was formerly the site of a Benedictine priory, founded in the reign of Henry I by Baldwin de Redvers, as a cell of the Norman monastery of Montburgh. It was dissolved as an alien house in 1411, and none of the original premises survived. But aspects of the picturesque church of St Magdalene, whose proportions and masonry show its Saxonand Norman origin appear to indicate that it may have been connected to the priory.

Bradpole, The Village 1902 48408
The tower and spire of Holy Trinity Church dominates this view of the little village north of Bridport, through which King Charles II passed on his flight after the calamitous Battle of Worcester in September 1651. A tablet in the church commemorates the event.

Walditch, The Village 1899 43879
The medieval system of strip-lynchet farming is still visible on the hillsides around this small hamlet in this turn of the century photograph. The small church of St Mary with its bellcote, on the lower right, was built in 1863.

Shipton Gorge, The Village 1899 43880
With a brick-built outhouse prominent in the foreground, and the Perpendicular west tower of St Martin's church to the right, this lofty view of the slate and thatched roofs of the winding village street along the valley bottom appears to be the photographer's attempt to make this place live up to its name. In fact, Gorge was the family surname of a succession of local squires, one of whom was severely wounded in a fierce action at Abbotsbury during the Civil War.

West Bay, from the West 1902 48402
Looking along the broad sweep of Lyme Bay toward the eminence of Barton Cliff, with the protective harbour walls jutting out to sea, and the signal mast of the coastguard station clearly visible. Inside the harbour itself, on the left, the mast of several sailing vessels rise above the surrounding buildings.

West Bay, The Harbour Entrance 1904 52763

West Bay, The Harbour Entrance 1904 52764
This spectacular swell, stirred up by the prevailing south-westerly winds, demonstrates not only the need for the massive solidity of these stone and wooden jetties against the power of the sea, but also gives a good impression of the difficulties faced by the masters of sailing vessels in negotiating the narrow entrance to the harbour, particularly in times of heavy weather.

West Bay
The Harbour 1899 43877
This artificial harbour, first
constructed between 1740-
44, stands at the estuary of
the small River Brit. It was
reconstructed in 1844, but
a harbour had existed here
for several centuries. Joan of
Navarre landed here in 1403
on her way to marry Henry IV.
The imposing terrace of five
tall houses, with a tile-hung
mansard roof at three levels,
had been built around 1885
by E S Prior, and the heaps of
stone on the other side of the
harbour may have been left
over after its construction, or
have been used as ballast by
sailing vessels visiting here.

◄ **West Bay**
The Coastguard Station 1907
58154
This small thatched building, with its telegraph connection standing alongside, faces towards the sea. Its Victorian and Edwardian staff would have been very occupied in monitoring the substantial shipping traffic in the treacherous waters of Lyme Bay, where in severe south-westerly storms many vessels, unable to weather the turbulent waters off Portland Bill, were swept to their doom on the Chesil Bank.

▼ **Chideock**
The Village 1903 50489
Situated in one of the most picturesque valleys in this part of the county, and spelled as Cidihoc in the Domesday Book, this peaceful view of the village street lined with well-built cob and sandstone cottages precedes the arrival of the motor vehicle, and the transformation of this thoroughfare into the busy A35. On the left is the mainly Perpendicular church of St Giles, restored in 1883 by Crickmay, who also built the chancel.

◄ **Seatown**
General View 1902 48415
This little group of cottages belonging to the fishermen whose boats are lined up on the foreshore, grew up around the declivity where the local stream, the Wynreford, after passing through Chideock, finally reaches the sea on this shingle beach. A fair used to be held here on Whit Monday and, from a cottage next to the local inn The Anchor, furmity (a sugar sweetened Dorset dish composed of wheat, raisins, and currants spiced with, often smuggled, spirits) was reputedly sold in the 19th century.

◄ **Bridport
East Street Station
1904** 52757
The railway first came
to Bridport in 1855,
passing through on its
way on a branch line
from Maiden Newton
to the terminus at West
Bay, a mile and a half to
the south.

Symondsbury
The Village & Church 1899 43871
Symondsbury is an intimate little village positioned between two rounded hills, and probably on the route of a medieval road linking Bridport and Axminster. The 14th- or 15th-century church of St John Baptist has a barrel roof, made by the shipwrights from West Bay which had been plastered over until the church was cleaned and renovated some 20 years after this picture was taken. To its right is Raymond's Charity School, built of yellow stone in 1868.

Bridport
Old Cottages 1897 40095
This seemingly idyllic rural summer scene on the banks of the River Brit, with its group of thatched cottages, lines of washing and vegetable garden, is brought acutely into focus by a closer inspection of the gable end of the nearest building. Part of the thatched roof on both sides is missing, exposing the underlying roof structure. This is probably due to an earlier fire in the chimneystack - one of the commonplace hazards of living in these picturesque structures.

Bridport
South Street 1897 40075
On the left, with its porch projecting into the street, is the 14th- or 15th-century Chantry House, while just beyond, a striped barber's pole overhanging the pavement indicates a gentlemen's hairdressing salon.
The tower of the 14th-century St Mary's Church, surprisingly positioned some way from the town centre, rises above the graceful Georgian frontages along this thoroughfare.

**Bridport
West Street 1902**
48390
The 18th-century
Town Hall, designed by
William Tyler, with its
small cupola and clock
added around the turn
of that century, stands
at the junction of the
town's three main
streets whose surprising
breadth is an indication
of Bridport's medieval
prosperity.

**Bridport
West Street 1909**
61645
The elegant mid-18th-century frontage of W Frost's printing business, with its Venetian-styled central window on the first floor, stands out amongst this varied collection of architectural styles as West Street slopes downhill towards the suburb of Allington.

J.J.SHEPHARD'
BRUSH&BASKE
MANUFACTOR
W.SHEPHARD'
PHOTOGRAPHI
ESTABLISHMEN

Bridport
East Street 1897 40073
With their awnings
fluttering in the summer
breeze, blowing in from
the hills beyond, the
shops on the far side
of the street await their
customers, while on
the shadowed side of
this broad thoroughfare,
a workman commences
his ascent of a ladder
to the roof above, and
a pony and cart
wait patiently at the
kerbside.

Dorchester & Weymouth

Burton Bradstock
The Village 1897 40086a
This charming village at the mouth of the River Bride, or Bredy, at
one time formed part of a manor which belonged to Bradenstock
Priory; hence the Bradstock of its name. It had been given by
Henry I to the abbey of St Stephen's at Caen in Normandy, in
exchange for the Crown regalia. Midway along this row of thatched
cottages is the bay window of the village shop.

Litton Cheney, The Village 1906 54545
The pretty, secluded village is still unspoilt, more than 90 years after this picture was taken. It was once the home of the noted typographer and engraver Reynolds Stone, who depicted the area in a series of watercolours and woodcuts. The three young girls seated on the bank, and the nearby boy, would undoubtedly have been able to sample the famous and authentic Blue Vinny cheese which, at the time of this photograph, was sold at the local post office.

Puncknowle, The Village 1906 54548
Under the spreading chestnut trees of St Mary's churchyard, and on the opposite side of the village street, the photographer's activities generate much interest from a mixed audience of both children and adults. The Napier family were, for three centuries until the early part of the 18th, lords of the manor here. A subsequent tenant of the manor house by the church, was Colonel Shrapnel, whose name is forever associated with his explosive invention.

Abbotsbury, The Tithe Barn 1890 27323
Part of the site of a Benedictine Abbey founded by Orc, a house-carl or steward, to King Cnut around 1044. The great monastic barn, a 15th-century structure, measures some 276 feet by 31 feet, with its ground plan resembling that of a church with transepts.

Maiden Newton, The Village 1906 54560
The arrival of the turnpike in 1778, linking Dorchester with Somerset, had a profound effect on this village. It was paralleled 79 years later with the opening of the Wiltshire, Somerset & Weymouth railway line, and its branch line from here to Bridport and West Bay. The building of the station in the central foreground, and the construction of the railway itself, provided a number of secure jobs for labourers at a time of agricultural depression.

Maiden Newton, Riversdale 1906 54568
The limpid and tranquil waters of the River Frome pass by this brick and corrugated iron building, where it is joined by the Toller, or Hooke, stream. Although the local textile industry was in severe decline by the start of the 19th century, the mill here continued to manufacture carpets throughout the 20th century.

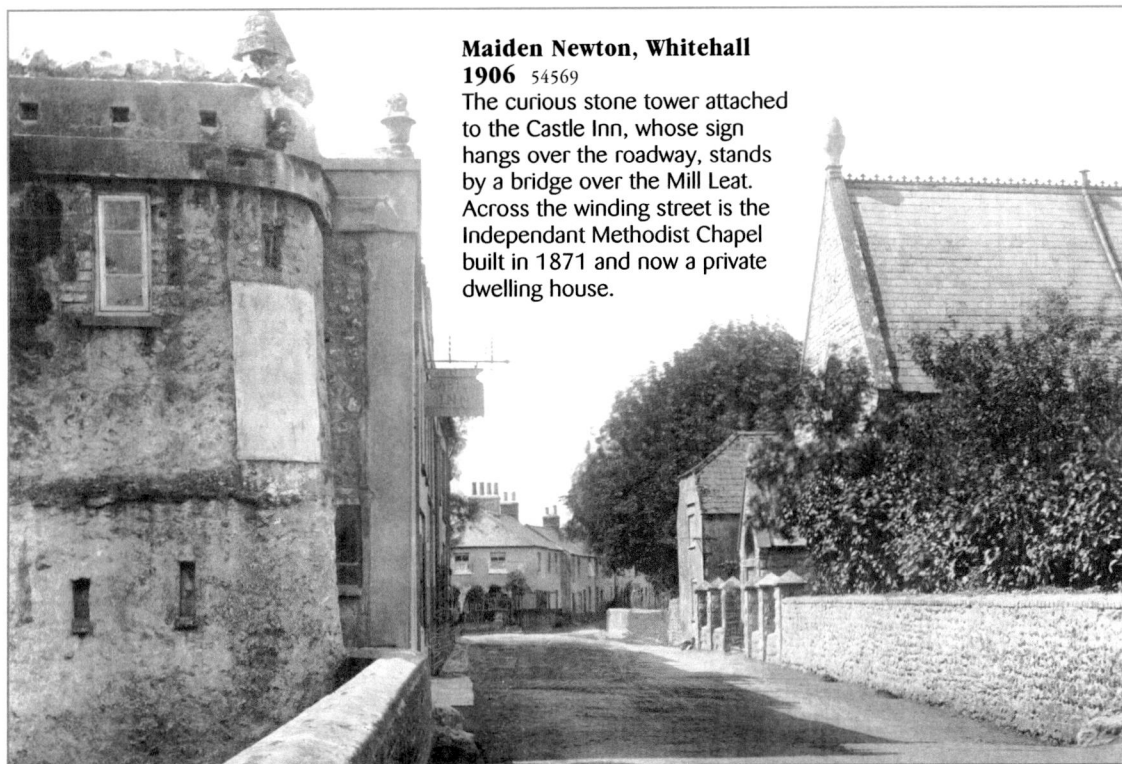

Maiden Newton, Whitehall 1906 54569
The curious stone tower attached to the Castle Inn, whose sign hangs over the roadway, stands by a bridge over the Mill Leat. Across the winding street is the Independant Methodist Chapel built in 1871 and now a private dwelling house.

▼ **Cattistock, The Village 1906** 54576

The 100-foot high slender stone tower of the church of St Peter and St Paul domi-nates this village built on a hairpin bend. Described by Pevsner as "the masterpiece among Dorset churches", it was rebuilt in 1857 by George Gilbert Scott, the son of the renowned Sir George Gilbert Scott. Its bell tower housed a carillon of 35 bells, cast at Louvain, and installed at a cost of more than £2,000. People would gather on the surrounding hills to listen to its peal.

▼ **Sydling St Nicholas, The Village 1910** 62580

On the left, the local postman wheels his bike along the High Street, while behind his companion's shoulder a laden horse-drawn hay wagon approaches. The entrance to the Victorian houses on the right, behind their wrought-iron railings, and the neighbouring Post Office, is gained by stepping over the stone slabs beneath which runs the Sydling stream.

▲ **Dorchester Higher West Street 1891** 28512x

This is the county town of Dorset, and the Casterbridge of Thomas Hardy's novels, viewed from the foot of Higher West Street with the spire of All Saints Church, the tower of St Peter's Church and the Town Hall clock turret dominating the skyline. Behind the stationary vehicles on the left are the offices of the architect John Hicks, where Hardy worked for a time.

◀ **Dorchester
St Peter's Church 1891**
28520
Positioned at the centre
of the town, where North,
South, West and East Streets
all meet, St Peter's was the
only church to survive
the fire which ravaged the
town in 1613. It is mainly
15th-century, but with this
13th-century south entrance.
Just visible behind the
lantern-topped gateway is
the statue of the poet William
Barnes, who wrote in Dorset
dialect, and who lived in
Dorchester from 1847 until
his death in 1886.

Upwey
The Wishing Well
1894 34554a
English's Wishing Well
and Tea Gardens,
situated at the foot of
a hill where the little
River Wey rises, were
a major attraction for
Victorian and Edwardian
visitors to Weymouth.
No holiday could be
considered complete
without participating
in a horse-drawn
wagonette ride to
the well for a shilling,
followed by a
strawberry tea.
The visitor would have
received his glass from
the apron-wearing
custodian and, after
making his wish and
drinking, emptied the
rest by throwing it
over his left shoulder.
Most important of all,
he would have then
have made his offering
of money to the keeper
of the well.

◄ **Radipole**
The Old Manor House
1894 34556a
A distinguished 16th-
and early 17th-century
three-storey building,
which incorporates part
of an earlier structure,
and stands close to the
eastern wall of St Ann's
Church. Its mullioned
windows and gables
appear in danger of
being swamped by
the luxuriant creepers
festooned across its
stone walls.

◄ **Upwey**
St Lawrence's Church &
Village c1870 8058
Positioned cosily beneath
the downs, and with its
cluster of thatched and
slate-roofed cottages
around it, the Perpendicular
west tower of this
surprisingly large church
rises above the surrounding
gravestones. The chancel
was rebuilt in 1906, but the
north aisle and arcade are
late Perpendicular.

▼ **Radipole**
St Ann's Church 1898 41134
The tower, with its triple
bellcote dates from the
early 16th century, but the
windows in the north transept
apparently date back to
the 13th century. The tall
chimneys of the Manor House
can be seen rising behind the
church itself.

◄ **Weymouth**
Swans 1890 27321
These graceful mature
birds are swimming in
the East Fleet, the long
lagoon which extends
behind the Chesil Beach
to the swannery at
Abbotsbury. The viaduct
behind them carries the
Weymouth and Portland
railway across this lagoon
from Wyke Regis to
the village of Easton on
Portland. It was opened
in 1857, and served for
the transportation of
stone from the quarries
on the island.

◄ **Weymouth
Sandsfoot Castle 1894**
34548
The Isle of Portland
looms out of the sea
mist, beyond the
warships at anchor in
the harbour. Henry VIII
built Sandsfoot Castle
in 1539 to protect this
natural anchorage, and
it was described by the
contemporary chronicler
and antiquary Leland
as "a right goodlie
Castel, having one open
barbicane".

◄ **Weymouth**
The Esplanade & Jubilee
Clock Tower 1890 27313
The Jubilee Clock was belatedly
installed on Weymouth's
seafront in 1888, a year after
the celebrations marking Queen
Victoria's Golden Jubilee. The
stone platform was installed on
the beach, but the subsequent
extension of the Esplanade
towards the sea in the 1920s
surrounded and covered the
base of the clock.

▼ **Weymouth**
The Harbour 1898 41110
Viewed from The Nothe, the majestic,
curving sweep of Weymouth seafront
can be seen behind the two paddle
steamers moored next to each other.
These vessels had been a traditional part
of holidays here from 1845 onwards,
when Captain Cosens first introduced
the first of his fleet of pleasure boats,
conveying trippers on excursions to
Portland Harbour, Lulworth Cove,
Swanage, Bournemouth, the Isle of
Wight, and even westwards to Torquay.
At the harbour station to the left, open
wagons await the arrival of the steamer
from the Channel Isles.

◄ **Weymouth**
The Jersey Boat 1898 41127
With a following wind, the boat
linking Weymouth and the
Channel Isles heads out from
the Dorset coast, while two
pleasure yachts head towards
Weymouth Harbour. The modest
size of this twin-funnelled steam
cargo and passenger boat offers
a remarkable contrast to the
substantial cross-Channel ferries
which took over this essential
service, and the massive roll-on-
roll-off car ferries which followed
them 75 years after this picture
was taken.

**Weymouth
The Esplanade 1898**

41116x

Everyone in this picture appears overdressed by today's standards for a day at the seaside. Weymouth's popularity as a resort remained high throughout the Victorian era, with substantial redevelopment taking place along the seafront. The cast iron and glass shelters with their small balconies extending over the beach were erected in the 1880s.

Weymouth, The Esplanade 1898 41123
This view shows the eastern end of the Esplanade with the imposing frontage and portico of the Imperial Burdon Hotel, later renamed the Prince Regent Hotel, on Victoria Terrace to the left. The spire of St John's Church, designed and built in 1850-54 by Talbot Bury, marks the start of the road to Dorchester, eight miles away.

Weymouth, The Sands 1904 52859
With the grand façade of the newly-constructed Royal Hotel in the background, replacing the simpler building which had been demolished in 1981, the ever-popular and long suffering Weymouth donkeys prepare to set off on another trek along the sands. To the extreme left are some of the miniature decorated landaus which were pulled by equally stoical goats.

Weymouth, The Esplanade 1909 61589x
Parked in front of one of the shelters, whose filigree ironwork can be clearly seen, these two cars must have been among the earliest motor vehicles to appear in Dorset. Their novelty value probably accounts for the fact that they are available for hire to holidaymakers for return trips to nearby Preston, only three miles distant, at the then substantial cost of 6d.

Osmington Mills, The Village 1894 34557
This small picturesque hamlet of thatched whitewashed cottages stands on the coast, alongside a stream running to the sea. Four miles from Weymouth, and with its Smuggler's Inn famed for its lobsters and prawns, it was a popular destination for walkers making use of the cliff path during the Victorian and Edwardian eras.

Portland, Chesil Beach 1877 9614

Portland, Chesil Beach 1890 27327

This is a spectacular view from the top of Portland, with the expanse of the Chesil Bank on the left, stretching 16 miles along the Dorset coast to Barton Cliff, and the broad expanse of Portland Harbour to the right with the Weymouth suburbs beyond. The fishing boats drawn up on the steep shingle bank at Chesilton are clearly visible, while the island's main village of Fortune's Well is immediately ahead. The great blocks of quarried stone, some 70,000 tons of which were transported from here annually, were utilised not only in the construction of many famous buildings in London from the time of James I, but also in the breakwater enclosing Portland harbour. It took 23 years to build, using mainly convict labour from the Verne Prison on the island, cost £1m, and was formally opened in 1872. It remains one of the largest naval harbours in the world.

Inland Dorset

Canford Magna, The Village 1904 52484
This shows part of the 800 acres of parkland surrounding Canford Manor, acquired in the middle of the
19th century by Sir John Guest, the grandson of a Shropshire iron master. It then became the seat of his son,
Lord Wimborne, and as can be seen, was meticulously maintained in Victorian philanthropic style.

▼ **Wimborne Minster, from the River 1899** 43715
Across the River Stour, the pinnacles of the Norman cruciform Minster rise from
the water meadows. The earliest religious house here was a nunnery founded by
Cuthberga, the sister of King Ina, between 704 -723. The Danes destroyed it in the
late 10th century. Edward the Confessor created a college of secular canons here,
and the church dates from this period of the 12th century.

▼ **Wimborne Minster, St Margaret's Church & Almshouses 1908** 60634
A little outside the town, this venerable institution was probably founded in the
13th century following Pope Innocent IV's papal indulgence for charitable offerings
and, like many others, set apart for lepers. John Redcoddes (or Redcotte) founded
a well-endowed chantry in the chapel, to the right, in Henry IV's reign. These
residents of the charitable almshouses appear content with their well-maintained
facilities and small central garden.

▲ **Wimborne Minster
West Borough 1908**
60623
With the towers of
the Minster in the
background, this street
lined with red brick
and white-rendered
Georgian cottages has
a pleasing elegance and
symmetry. Among the
more imposing buildings
away from the camera
are the premises of the
Wimborne Club and, on
the opposite side of the
street, the Wimborne
Conservative Club.

◀ **Wimborne Minster
The Grammar School
1886** 19489
Morris & Ebson constructed
this gaudy building, of
red brick and Bath stone,
between 1849-51, in the
style of Henry VII, whose
mother Margaret, Countess
of Richmond, founded the
seminary at Wimborne. In
the reign of Elizabeth I, a
Royal Charter converted
it into Queen Elizabeth's
Grammar School.

**Wimborne Minster
The Coach & Horses
1908** 60637
With a pony and
trap halted outside
the thatched inn,
the photographer's
activity appears to have
fascinated everyone
in the vicinity, with
the exception of the
two canines. The little
boy in his straw boater
and smock has found
himself a comfortable
perch on the railings
leading to the water
meadows.

Wimborne St Giles, The River Allen from East Brook Bridge 1908 60627
The River Allen rises to the south west of Cranborne, near this well-preserved 17th-century brick millhouse, and under the bridge into the park of St. Giles House. It then makes its way through the meadows for ten miles to join the River Stour at Wimborne Minster.

Colehill, The Firs 1908 60638
North of Wimborne, and once part of the ancient parish of Holt, Colehill is in the area of the Deserta, where heaths and woodland form the predominant feature of the landscape. The matronly lady in her apron talking to the two young girls seated at the roadside, and clutching a staff, may have been gathering pine cones from the surrounding trees for use as kindling.

Crichel House, The House & Park 1904 52752
The original house, owned by the Napier family, burnt down in 1742, and the wealthy Humphrey Sturt, who had married an heiress, inherited the estate in 1765. He at once embarked on a programme of rebuilding and extension, doubling the size of the house, and moved the entire village of More Crichel except for St Mary's Church, a mile away to the south in order to landscape the surrounding park. The displaced inhabitants were rehoused in a new village at Newtown, in the parish of Witchampton.

Kingston Lacy
The House 1899 43720
The old lords of Kingston were the Norman nobles, the Lacys, but this palatial Restoration house was built in 1663-5 for Sir Ralph Bankes, the son of the former attorney general Sir John. It was extensively modified and augmented between 1835-46 by Sir Charles Barry, at the behest of W J Bankes, the friend of Lord Byron, who had amassed a superb collection of paintings and wished to show them to their best advantage.

◀ **Crichel House**
White Farm 1904 52753
These goats and cattle, watched over by their proud custodian, are representative of a fashion indulged in by many major landowners during the 19th century for breeding and raising unusual animals on their extensive properties. Humphrey Sturt in particular, had many ideas for the advancement of agriculture, not only here but also on Brownsea Island in Poole Harbour which he brought under cultivation.

▼ **Witchampton**
The Village 1904 52740
Beyond the ornamental lych gate framed by these cottages is the church of St Mary and St Cuthberga, whose brown and grey stone west tower is Perpendicular. The remainder of the building is Victorian, dating from 1844.

◀ **Witchampton**
The Mill 1904 52742
A discreet industrial intrusion into this agricultural plain on the River Allen, this paper mill had been in operation for more than 100 years when this photograph was taken, and continues up to the present day.

Witchampton, The Village 1904 52741
The winding street of this secluded village, with its magnificent trees, tiled and thatched cottages and well-kept gardens must have provided a wonderful playground for the children seen lined up on the far side of the road.

▲ **Sherborne**
The Old Castle Courtyard 1886 13847

◄ **Sherborne**
The Old Castle Gate House 1886
13845
The castle was built by Roger of Caen,
the Baron-Bishop of Salisbury in the reign
of Henry I and, with the manor, attached
to the see of Old Sarum and Salisbury.
A palace rather than a fortress, in the late
16th century, Elizabeth sub-let it to
Sir Walter Raleigh who began converting
it as his mansion. But it was finally
reduced to a ruin during the Civil War,
after it was taken by the Parliamentary
forces under Sir Thomas Fairfax on 16
August 1645.

Sherborne, The Conduit 1887 19669
The hexagonal conduit stands in the tiny square before the eastern gateway to the Abbey precinct. Abbot Mere built it in the early 16th century as the lavatorium in the Abbey cloister.

Sherborne, Cheap Street 1891 29652
Beside the lamp standard at the conduit, and with Cheap Street extending beyond, a small pony enjoys a welcome snack, as it stands harnessed to its two-wheeled trap, awaiting the return of its owner.

Sherborne, Long Street 1891 29653
The soaring Gothic of the Abbey Church, transformed from its late Norman structure into Perpendicular style, dominates the skyline of this shaded street leading up to the old castle, with the Castle Hotel and the Rose and Crown Inn on the right. The tower of the church had undergone substantial restoration six years before this photograph was taken.

Sherborne, Castleton Church 1891 29656
St Mary Magdalene was consecrated in 1715, and was designed by the 5th Lord Digby, who resided at Sherborne Castle, and whose family were the second largest landowners in the county. In 1873, at the peak of their power, the Digbys controlled an estate of more than 20,000 acres in Dorset. The poet Alexander Pope was a great admirer of the "good Lord Digby" and expressed his approval of this building: "My lord modestly told me he was glad I liked it, because it was of his own architecture".

Sherborne, Horse and Cart 1904 51329x
In common with many shop-owners of the time, the tailors and outfitters Phillips and Handover displayed their wares not only in the windows of their premises, but also outside. The stockman's sturdy coats on offer here would havecost an agricultural labourer more than a week's wages to buy.

Purbeck & Poole

Wool
Woolbridge Manor 1904 52731
Set beside the five-arched stone bridge across the River Frome,
the 17th-century manor was once the home of the Turberville
family, and is immortalised in Thomas Hardy's novel. On a
landing inside this mellow stone and brick building with its three
prominent chimneys are the wall paintings which frightened
'Tess of the D'Urbervilles' on her honeymoon here with
Angel Clare. At the start of the Edwardian period it was still a
farmhouse, but has since
become a luxury hotel.

West Lulworth, The Village 1904 52710
This little village encompassed by hills stretches along the minor road leading on to Lulworth Cove. At the extreme left are the local Lulworth Stores, with window blinds half-lowered to protect its displayed wares, while on the bend leading to the sea is the Cove Hotel. The promontory to the extreme right was the original site chosen by the Cistercians for the foundation of Bindon Abbey in 1150, and is now occupied by a cottage.

West Lulworth, the Village 1903 49143
The village street curves around the foot of Bindon Hill as it approaches the cove, with the Cove Hotel next to the thatched cottages on the left. Behind is the church of the Holy Trinity, rebuilt in 1869-70 by the Weymouth architect John Hicks.

West Lulworth, The Village 1904 52709
A group of carefully constructed haystacks, in this stackyard at the end of the village, await the oncoming winter when they would provide fodder for cattle and horses. This late summer scene belies the harsh winters that might follow,when remote villages like this could find themselves cut off from their neighbouring towns for several weeks at a time.

Lulworth, The Cove 1894 34581
The entrance to this circular natural basin is barely discernible from the sea, guarded as it is by two projecting spurs of resistant Portland and Purbeck strata. Inside, the constant action of the waves has eroded the nearly vertical and contorted beds of chalk and Hastings sand, to create this 500-yard lagoon. As well as the small local fishing boats pictured here, it was also a popular destination for the Victorian paddle steamers from nearby Weymouth, which had specially strengthened bows to enable the vessel to be run up onto the beach and disembark passengers.

Lulworth, The Castle Inn 1903 49145
An Edwardian gentleman in his straw boater gazes down on this little group of thatched cottages surrounding the creeper-clad Castle Inn, whose turnover must have benefited enormously from the hordes of day trippers visiting this local beauty spot during the summer months. The carefully tended vegetable garden ascending the hill behind shows how important self-sufficiency was in these remote hamlets, in the days before motor vehicles and supermarkets.

Warbarrow, The Bay c1877 9606
The rowing boats and solitary figure standing on the isolated shingle beach offer a rare glimpse of what is now part of the Army's prohibited Lulworth Range. About 1,000 acres of land, extending five miles along the coast and five miles northwards, were taken over by the military during World War Two, and have yet to be returned to the public. But the local wildlife has benefited in spite of the tanks and artillery, and the area is now Dorset's most outstanding refuge.

East Lulworth, The Village 1904 52722

East Lulworth, The Village 1904 52724
Three miles inland from the cove, this little collection of 18th-century thatched or tiled cottages formed part of the neighbouring manor estate, originally owned by the Newborowes. Leland visited here in Henry VIII's reign and wrotethat "about East Lilleworth is metely good ground and plenty of wood".

East Lulworth, The Weld Arms Inn 1904 52720
The Weld family, whose genealogy can be traced back to Edrike the Wild, or Welde, through King Elthelred, are Dorset's leading Roman Catholic, or recusant, family. They have owned the estate here since 1641, and their escutcheon adorns the local pub. Thomas Weld entertained George III to dinner here at Lulworth Castle, during one of the monarch's visits to Weymouth, and, having served him with food on gold and silver plates and arranged for the 15 Weld children to sing 'God Save The King', obtained royal permission to build a Roman Catholic church for the family's use.

Corfe Castle, The Village 1890 25582
The strategic importance of the site is apparent in this view from the ruins of the castle on its mound. Below, the village, built largely of Purbeck stone, clusters around St Edward's Church, built in 1859-60, but with elements of its original Norman structure embodied in it.

Corfe Castle, East Street 1899 43784
The magnificent ruins of the castle glower down on these little stone cottages. Originally probably a Saxon fortification, it was expanded during the Norman Conquest and King John made it a royal residence and prison. Besieged during the Civil War, it was delivered by treachery into the hands of the Parliamentarians, and subsequently mined and blasted into its existing state.

Kingston, The Church 1899 43788
Built by the 3rd Earl of Eldon at an estimated cost of £70,000, the church of St James was constructed between 1873-80. Its massive central tower is visible for miles around and is disproportionate both to the remainder of the building, and to the small village it was intended to serve, although considered one of the masterpieces of its architect G E Street.

Worth Matravers, St Nicholas Church 1899 43791
This early Norman church is dedicated to the patron saint of sailors, St Nicholas of Myra, and was restored by the Earl of Eldon. Its churchyard contains the tomb of Benjamin Jesty who died in 1816. He was "noted for being the first person (known) that introduced the cow-pox by inoculation, and who from his great strength of mind made theexperiment from the cow on his Wife and two Sons in the year 1774".

St Alban's Head & Bottom Valley 1899 43789
Alternatively known as St Aldhem's Head, after the famous first bishop of Sherborne, this bold promontory, 353 feet high, is the most southerly point of the Isle of Purbeck, and is reached along this winding road at the foot of the valley. A small quarry produced Purbeck stone for the replacement and repair of ornamental work in churches.

Swanage, The Beach & Grand Hotel 1899 43768
Snug between the two headlands of Ballard Point and Peverel Point, the broad sweep of Swanage Bay proved so popular with visitors during the late 19th century that it rapidly grew from a village of stone cottages to a red brick town of big hotels and gabled, turreted villas. Featured in the Domesday Book as Swanic, in earlier days it was a favourite landing place of marauding Danes, and the scene of King Alfred's great naval victory over them in 877.

Swanage, The Promenade 1897 40302
A visit by Princess Victoria in 1835 helped to stimulate interest in Swanage as a resort, but it was the activities of the general contractor and collector George Burt, the controlling mind behind the boarding house boom of the 1880s, and his uncle John Mowlem, who jointly gave the town its muddled architectural character. By 1897 the process of development was in full swing and, beyond the row of bathing machines, many of the new buildings gleam in the sun.

COMPARATIVE SIZES OF THE SUN MOON AND PLANETS, ON THE SAME SCALE AS THIS GLOBE, WHICH IS TEN FEET DIAMETER		MEAN DIAMETER OF THE SUN, MOON AND PLANETS, IN MILES	
	FEET. INS		
THE SUN WOULD BE	1090 - 0	866.400	
JUPITER	109 - 0	86.500	
SATURN	92 - 0	73.000	
NEPTUNE	44 - 0	34.800	8
URANUS	40 - 0	31.900	26,
THE EARTH	10 - 0	7.918	174
VENUS	9 - 3	7.700	24
MARS	5 - 4	4.200	24
MERCURY	4 - 0	3.000	36.
THE MOON	2 - 9	2.160	47.0
			2

ABOVE SEA 136 FT

Text visible on the globe:

IN THE SOLAR
AND IS THE

00.000 MILES.
THE VERNAL
SEPTEMBER 21

2,160 MILES.
.600 MILES.
W (28 DAYS), AND
ENCE VERY NEARLY
WAYS TURNED TOWARDS

THE EARTH PRODUCES
MOON BEING ABOUT
SUN.

ARS.
THE NEAREST FIXED STAR
SOUTHERN HEMISPHERE, IS
S THAT OF THE SUN.
E RATE OF ABOUT 156,000 MILES IN
AND A HALF YEARS IN REACHING THE

Swanage
The Globe 1892 31357
Installed in the grounds
of Durlston Castle by
George Burt in 1890,
this 40-ton block of
Portland stone, ten feet
in diameter, incised with
representations of the
continents and place
names, was intended
to be educational
for Victorian visitors.
However, although
depicted on its correct
axis, the world has
changed so much that
much of the inscribed
information is now out
of date.

**Swanage
The Tilly Whim Caves
1890** 25551
A popular tourist
attraction around the
turn of the century,
but now no longer
open to the public,
the Tilly Whim Caves
on Durlston Head, and
below the lighthouse
perched on Anvil Point,
were once used by the
local Dorset smugglers
for storing contraband
away from the prying
eyes of Customs and
Excise officers.

Swanage, Studland Church Interior 1890 25556
Set among aged yew trees, the Norman church of St Nicholas was apparently built on the remains of an earlier Saxon church destroyed by the Danes in the 9th century. That, in turn, had been raised on the site of what was probably a pre-Christian temple. The 12th-century arches with decorated capitals separating the nave and chancel support the central tower, and the vaulted roof makes this one of the most complete Norman village churches.

Studland, The Sands 1899 43779
The vista of Studland Bay, with its curving sandy beach, is seen from Ballard Down. Beyond are Poole Bay and Harbour and the satellite suburbs of Bournemouth. Bracken and marram grass hold the sand dunes together, while closer to hand in the middle distance is Little Sea, a brackish lake which provides a sanctuary for waterfowl.

Studland, Cottages 1899 43780
Thatched roofs, leaded windows, local stone and a profusion of creepers and roses, set amid lofty trees, make this scene an archetypal image of countryside tranquillity. Even at the turn of the 19th century it must have struck a chord with visitors escaping from noisy, crowded Victorian cities and, as a holiday postcard or as a souvenir, proved immensely popular.

**Brownsea Island
The Castle 1891** 29624
Begun as a blockhouse to
protect Poole Harbour in
the reign of Henry VIII, it
was completed in 1547-
8. The remains of the
blockhouse survive only as
a basement room. It was
expanded over succeeding
centuries, most notably
by Colonel William Petrie
Waugh in the early 1850s.
This building burnt down
in 1896, but was
subsequently rebuilt.

◄ **Studland**
Bank's Hotel 1899 43782
Under the lee of Ballard Down, the undressed stone façade and slated roof of Blake's hotel was originally built around 1825 as a marine villa for the Rt Hon George Bankes, whose retirement pastime was enlarging the property. Later it was turned into an hotel, and is now the Manor House Hotel.

▼ **Sandbanks**
The Haven Hotel 46102
Standing on the slim, sandy peninsula jutting out from Poole Head, and facing the castle on Brownsea Island, this isolated hotel must have lived up to its name for those wanting to get away from it all. A ferry service operated from here to the island, and the narrow entrance to the harbour itself still provides close views of the shipping.

◄ **Poole**
Beech Hurst 1904 52809
At the top of the High Street stands this magnificent three-storey residence built in 1798 for the merchant Samuel Rolles, indicative of the wealth which came to the town in the 18th century, largely as a result of the Newfoundland fishing trade. The luxuriant creeper largely conceals its red brick exterior, but its crowning pediment proudly bears a coat of arms embraced by palm fronds.

Poole
Town Hall 1898 41165
Built in 1761, this was
the gift of the town's
seven members of
Parliament. The arcaded
ground floor was
never fully opened.
The grand entrance to
the council chamber
clearly provided a
model for that of the
later Georgian Custom
House, with two semi-
circular railed flights of
steps sweeping up to
the Tuscan pedimented
porch. Behind the
building are the arched
windows of the Police
Station.-

**Poole
Barges & Quay 1908**
61171
The substantial number of vessels moored alongside the quay gives an impression of the volume of shipping trade still enjoyed by Poole in the early years of the 20th century. Timber was a major import, accounting for more than half of the figure, while large quantities of china clay was the principal export.

Poole
Longfleet Road 1904
52810
The electric-trams, drawing their power from an overhead cable and following a track laid in the road surface, were introduced into Britain in the final decade of the Victorian era. Poole, along with other provincial towns and cities, quickly adopted this efficient and inexpensive, if noisy, form of public transport. They were eventually replaced by the motorbus which had the advantage of greater manoeuvrability.

Poole, The Park 1904 52803
The park was the result of an initiative of Lord Wimborne, supported by the local authorities. The parklands also included this saltwater lake covering 60 acres, with facilities for rowing and a resident population of swans and other wild fowl.

Parkstone, Sandecotes 1900 46098
Parkstone began as a ribbon development east of Poole, on the high ground north-east of the harbour. The large Victorian villas, set in spacious gardens which had once been heathland, proved to be extremely popular with new residents, and the start of the 20th century witnessed massive development in this area.

Index

FRITH PRODUCTS & SERVICES

Francis Frith would doubtless be pleased to know that the pioneering publishing venture he started in 1860 still continues today. Over a hundred and forty years later, The Francis Frith Collection continues in the same innovative tradition and is now one of the foremost publishers of vintage photographs in the world. Some of the current activities include:

INTERIOR DECORATION

Today Frith's photographs can be seen framed and as giant wall murals in thousands of pubs, restaurants, hotels, banks, retail stores and other public buildings throughout the country. In every case they enhance the unique local atmosphere of the places they depict and provide reminders of gentler days in an increasingly busy and frenetic world.

PRODUCT PROMOTIONS

Frith products are used by many major companies to promote the sales of their own products or to reinforce their own history and heritage. Frith promotions have been used by Hovis bread, Courage beers, Scots Porage Oats, Colman's mustard, Cadbury's foods, Mellow Birds coffee, Dunhill pipe tobacco, Guinness, and Bulmer's Cider.

GENEALOGY AND FAMILY HISTORY

As the interest in family history and roots grows world-wide, more and more people are turning to Frith's photographs of Great Britain for images of the towns, villages and streets where their ancestors lived; and, of course, photographs of the churches and chapels where their ancestors were christened, married and buried are an essential part of every genealogy tree and family album.

FRITH PRODUCTS

All Frith photographs are available Framed or just as Mounted Prints and Posters (size 23 x 16 inches). These may be ordered from the address below. Other products available are - Address Books, Calendars, Jigsaws, Canvas Prints, Postcards and local and prestige books.

THE INTERNET

Already ninety thousand Frith photographs can be viewed and purchased on the internet through the Frith websites and a myriad of partner sites.

For more detailed information on Frith products, look at this site:
www.francisfrith.com

See the complete list of Frith Books at: www.francisfrith.com
This web site is regularly updated with the latest list of publications from The Francis Frith Collection. If you wish to buy books relating to another part of the country that your local bookshop does not stock, you may purchase on-line.

For further information, trade, or author enquiries please contact us at the address below:
The Francis Frith Collection, Unit 6, Oakley Business Park, Wylye Road, Dinton, Wiltshire SP3 5EU.
Tel: +44 (0)1722 716 376 Fax: +44 (0)1722 716 881 Email: sales@francisfrith.co.uk

---

See Frith products on the internet at www.francisfrith.com

FREE PRINT OF YOUR CHOICE
CHOOSE A PHOTOGRAPH FROM THIS BOOK

+ £3.50 POSTAGE

Mounted Print
Overall size 14 x 11 inches (355 x 280mm)

TO RECEIVE YOUR FREE PRINT

Choose any Frith photograph in this book

Simply complete the Voucher opposite and return it with your remittance for £3.50 (to cover postage and handling) and we will print the photograph of your choice in SEPIA (size 11 x 8 inches) and supply it in a cream mount ready to frame (overall size 14 x 11 inches).

Order additional Mounted Prints
at HALF PRICE - £10.00 each (normally £20.00)

If you would like to order more Frith prints from this book, possibly as gifts for friends and family, you can buy them at half price (with no additional postage costs).

Have your Mounted Prints framed

For an extra £19.00 per print you can have your mounted print(s) framed in an elegant polished wood and gilt moulding, overall size 16 x 13 inches (no additional postage required).

IMPORTANT!

❶ Please note: aerial photographs and photographs with a reference number starting with a "Z" are not Frith photographs and cannot be supplied under this offer.

❷ Offer valid for delivery to one UK address only.

❸ These special prices are only available if you use this form to order. You must use the ORIGINAL VOUCHER on this page (no copies permitted). We can only despatch to one UK address.

❹ This offer cannot be combined with any other offer.

As a customer your name & address will be stored by Frith but not sold or rented to third parties. Your data will be used for the purpose of this promotion only.

Send completed Voucher form to:

The Francis Frith Collection,
6 Oakley Business Park, Wylye Road,
Dinton, Wiltshire SP3 5EU

Voucher for **FREE** and Reduced Price Frith Prints

Please do not photocopy this voucher. Only the original is valid, so please fill it in, cut it out and return it to us with your order.

Picture ref no	Page no	Qty	Mounted @ £10.00	Framed + £19.50	Total Cost £
		1	Free of charge*	£	£
			£10.00	£	£
			£10.00	£	£
			£10.00	£	£
			£10.00	£	£
			£10.00	£	£

Please allow 28 days for delivery.
Offer available to one UK address only

* Post & handling	£3.80
Total Order Cost	£

Title of this book . . . .

I enclose a cheque/postal order for £ . . . . made payable to 'The Francis Frith Collection'

OR please debit my Mastercard / Visa / Maestro card, details below

Card Number:

Issue No (Maestro only):   Valid from (Maestro):

Card Security Number: Expires:

Signature:

Name Mr/Mrs/Ms . . . .

Address . . . .

. . . .

. . . .

. . . . Postcode . . . .

Daytime Tel No . . . .

Email . . . .

Valid to 31/12/15

Free Print – see overleaf

Can you help us with information about any of the Frith photographs in this book?

We are gradually compiling an historical record for each of the photographs in the Frith archive. It is always fascinating to find out the names of the people shown in the pictures, as well as insights into the shops, buildings and other features depicted.

If you recognize anyone in the photographs in this book, or if you have information not already included in the author's caption, do let us know. We would love to hear from you, and will try to publish it in future books or articles.

An Invitation from The Francis Frith Collection to Share Your Memories

The 'Share Your Memories' feature of our website allows members of the public to add personal memories relating to the places featured in our photographs, or comment on others already added. Seeing a place from your past can rekindle forgotten or long held memories. Why not visit the website, find photographs of places you know well and add YOUR story for others to read and enjoy? We would love to hear from you!

www.francisfrith.com/memories

Our production team

Frith books are produced by a small dedicated team at offices near Salisbury. Most have worked with the Frith Collection for many years. All have in common one quality: they have a passion for the Frith Collection.

Frith Books and Gifts

We have a wide range of books and gifts available on our website utilising our photographic archive, many of which can be individually personalised.

www.francisfrith.com